TALKING LEAVES THE STORY OF SEQUOYAH

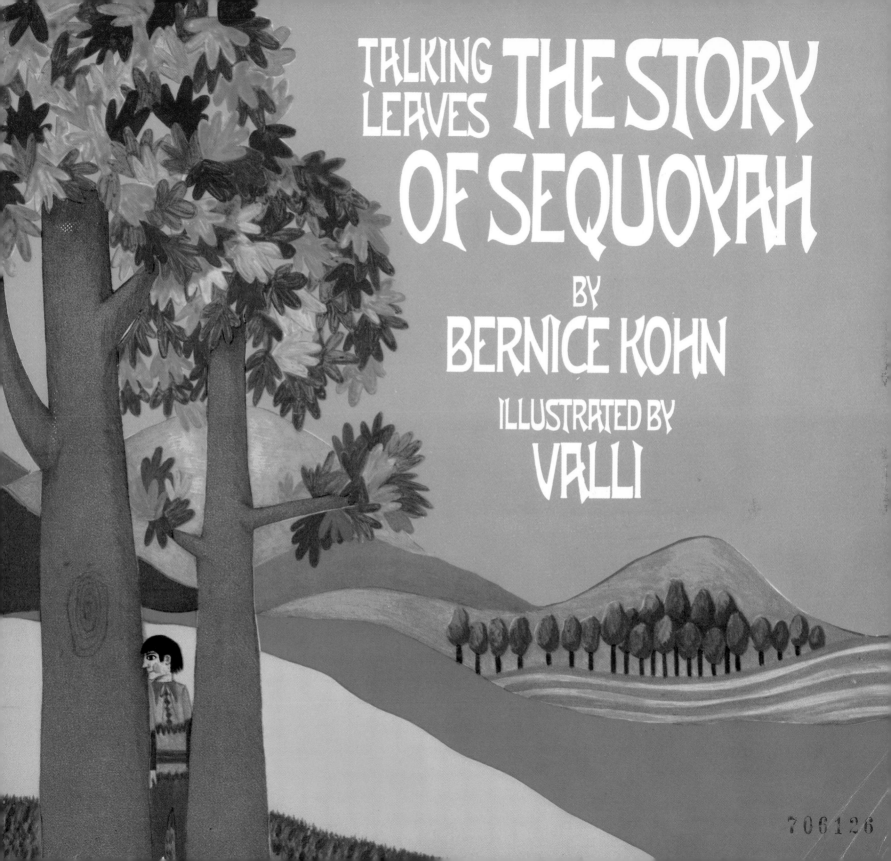

TALKING LEAVES THE STORY OF SEQUOYAH

BY BERNICE KOHN

ILLUSTRATED BY VALLI

A long time ago, when our country was young, there lived an Indian boy named Sequoyah.

He was not as tall as his friends and he walked with a limp. Yet this small lame boy grew up to be the greatest Cherokee of them all.

For it was Sequoyah who taught his people the secret of the talking leaves.

Sequoyah was born in the hills of Tennessee in about the year 1773. No one knows for sure just which year it was. In those days, the Indians could not read or write. They did not keep records of when people were born or when they died.

Sequoyah was part of a noble family on his mother's side. His grandfather was a great chief. His mother, Wuh-teh, was a royal princess of the Paint clan.

Sequoyah's father was a white man named Nathaniel Gist. He was a soldier, trader, and explorer. The Cherokees liked him so much that they let him marry Wuh-teh, even though she was a princess. They gave him one of their islands to live on. He stayed with the tribe for many years.

When Sequoyah was a baby, his father had to go back to his own people. His Indian family did not go with him. Sequoyah and his mother stayed with the tribe. This was the custom.

As a boy, Sequoyah almost died from the "green sickness" in his knee. After he got well one leg was weak and shorter than the other. He hunted less. He began to make use of his strong hands.

He started to paint animals and to carve them in wood. Soon he could carve the Golo masks that the braves wore.

Later he learned to make strong iron pots and pans for Wuh-teh.

By the time Sequoyah was a young man he was able to make fine jewelry. He made beautiful necklaces and bracelets for his young Cherokee bride. He also built her a log cabin and a spinning wheel with his own hands.

Sequoyah and his wife had five children. First four sons were born. Finally they had a daughter. The little girl was named Ah-yoka.

In 1812, Sequoyah heard that the United States was at war with England. He left his family to fight with the American soldiers.

In camp, Sequoyah tasted food and saw clothes that were strange to him. But strangest of all was the new language, English.

Then Sequoyah made a discovery that was to change his life and the lives of all the Cherokees. Sequoyah found out about reading and writing.

One day, Sequoyah saw a messenger hand the captain something that looked like a large white leaf. It was a piece of paper. Sequoyah saw that the "leaf" was covered with many black marks.

He watched the captain as he read the message. The captain nodded his head a few times and said, "Aha! We will just see about that!" To Sequoyah it seemed as though the little marks on the paper were *talking* to the Captain.

When the war was over, Sequoyah was very happy to return to his tribe. He had missed his family and friends.

Still, Sequoyah had not forgotten the mystery of the talking leaves. He decided that if it was possible to make leaves talk, then he, Sequoyah, would make them talk for the Cherokee people.

Sequoyah tried to make a picture sign for every word he could think of. He drew the signs on bark with a lump of charcoal. He drew picture signs for horses and fires and chickens and pots and arrows and every other thing he knew. In a very short time, he had thousands of signs. Who could remember them all? Even Sequoyah was getting mixed up—and he had just begun. There had to be a better way.

The Cherokee Alphabet

vowels — D a D e R e i T ꭳ o u O v i

sounds

g G g Ꮖ ga Ꮙ ka Ᏸ ge Ᏹ gi A go Ꭻ gu E gv

h Ꭽ ha Ᏺ ha Ꮅ he Ꭿ hi Ꮠ ho Ꮡ hu Ꮣ hv

L l l Ꮃ la Ꮄ le Ꮅ li Ꮆ lo M lu Ꮈ lv

m Ꮉ ma Ꮊ me Ꮋ mi Ꮌ mo Ꮍ mu

N Ꮎ na Ꮏ hna Ꮐ nah Ꮑ ne Ꮒ ni Ꮓ no Ꮔ nu Ꮕ nv

q q q Ꮖ qua Ꮗ que Ꮘ qui Ꮙ quo Ꮚ quu

s Ꮝ s s Ꭱ quv Ꮼ s Ꮜ sa Ꮞ se Ꮟ si Ꮠ so Ꮡ su Ꮢ sv

D d Ꮣ da Ꮤ ta Ꮥ de Ꮦ te Ꮧ di Ꮨ ti Ꮩ do Ꮪ du Ꮫ dv

T t t Ꮬ dla Ꮭ tla Ꮮ tle Ꮯ tli Ꮰ tlo Ꮱ tlu Ꮲ tlv

Ꮳ Ꮳ tsa Ꮴ tse Ꮵ tsi Ꮶ tso Ꮷ tsu Ꮸ tsv

w W W � wa Ꮻ we Ꮼ wi Ꮽ wo Ꮾ wu Ꮿ wv

y Ᏸ ya Ᏹ ye Ᏺ yi Ᏻ yo Ᏼ yu B yv

Sequoyah's "talking leaves"

Sequoyah thought and thought—and then one day the idea came. Of course! All words are made up of sounds. He didn't need a sign for every word but only for every sound. By putting the sounds together, any word could be formed.

Sequoyah set to work right away to find out how many sounds there were in the Cherokee language. He spoke each sound out loud so he could really hear it. His friends began to look at him strangely. They thought he was talking to himself!

Then Sequoyah found a child's spelling book. At last he held in his own hands the white man's talking leaves. Perhaps he could learn the magic. He decided to copy some of the letters on bark. Several of them looked prettier upside down or sideways, so he drew them that way instead.

Sequoyah began to work night and day. The pile of bark sheets grew higher and higher. But Sequoyah wasn't interested in anything else, not even the farming.

The medicine man could not understand what Sequoyah was doing. He began to speak against Sequoyah. He said that Sequoyah was making bad magic for the tribe. Sequoyah's wife became angry at Sequoyah because no one liked him anymore. She swept up all the pieces of bark and threw them into the fire.

At first Sequoyah was very upset, but soon he started to work all over again. At last Sequoyah was finished. He had made a sign for each of the syllables in the Cherokee language. Sequoyah had invented a syllabary, which is very like an alphabet.

An alphabet has a sign for every sound in the language. A syllabary has a sign for every syllable. There were eighty-six signs in Sequoyah's syllabary.

But now what? Could other Cherokees learn to use the syllabary? Little Ah-yoka could already read and write. But what about the others? Would they care? Would they *want* to learn?

Sequoyah decided to find out if all the years of hard work had been worthwhile. It was 1821 and it was time to make a test.

Sequoyah went to the head of the Cherokee Tribal Council who called a meeting. Word of Sequoyah's talking leaves spread like wildfire through the tribe. The Council room was soon jammed with excited people.

Sequoyah was sent out of the room. He was guarded by two warriors. They made sure that Sequoyah could not hear what was happening in the Council Chamber.

Inside, the most important chiefs gave messages to Ah-yoka. Nothing could be heard in the room but the scratching of the little girl's quill pen.

At last Sequoyah was called back into the room. He strode up to Ah-yoka, took the paper from her hand and read what she had written in a clear, loud voice. The room burst into a roar. It worked! The Cherokee nation had a written language at last!

Now everyone wanted to learn the new syllabary at once. Little children and wise old men studied together. There were Cherokees who had struggled for years to learn how to spell their names and a few other words of English. To them Sequoyah's syllabary seemed like a miracle. Many of them were reading and writing in a few weeks.

During the next year, Sequoyah helped to train many Cherokee teachers because everyone wanted to learn to read and write. Soon Cherokees everywhere were writing letters telling far-away friends about a new baby or the death of an old person. They also wrote poems and thank-you letters to their friends.

By 1828 the Cherokee nation had its own newspaper, the *Cherokee Phoenix*. Books were printed on the nation's own press. There was a Cherokee magazine and a Cherokee Bible. Schools were opened where Cherokee children did not have to learn the English ABC's. They learned to read and write in their own language.

Of course everyone was very proud of Sequoyah. Never before had just one man made up a written language by himself! Sequoyah was honored by all Americans, not just the Cherokees.

Even the President of the United States heard of what Sequoyah had done. To show how proud he was of Sequoyah, he gave him a gift. He was to receive $500.00 a year for the rest of his life. In those days, $500.00 was a great deal of money. This was the first literary prize given to anyone in the United States.

But the gift that pleased Sequoyah most was a beautiful silver medal with his picture on it. It was given to him by his own people. He proudly wore the medal around his neck for the rest of his life.

Sequoyah lived in Oklahoma now. He was an important man in his tribe and in the nation. He was called to Washington to talk with the President about his people. His portrait was painted.

Still Sequoyah often thought about making the syllabary even better.

When he heard about some Cherokees in Mexico, he wondered if they could use the syllabary, too. He decided to go and look for them.

Sequoyah set out for Mexico in 1842, when he was about seventy years old. It was a long and difficult trip on foot and on horseback, much too hard a trip for an old man in poor health.

Shortly after he arrived in Mexico in 1843, Sequoyah became very sick and died. He was buried in a secret place with his beloved medal.

The Cherokee people and the whole nation were unhappy. Everyone knew they had lost a very great and wise man.

Today a statue of Sequoyah stands in the Hall of Fame. It reminds us of the simple man who brought a great gift to his people—the written word.

The tallest trees in the world, the giant redwoods, are called sequoias. They are named for the small lame boy who became the greatest Cherokee of them all—a giant among his people.